Crushing The Competition

The Entrepreneur's Guide To Using Military Strategies To Outthink, Outmaneuver and Outperform The Competition

Omar Johnson

Copyright 2013 by Omar Johnson. Published by Make Profits Easy LLC

Profitsdaily123@aol.com

facebook.com/MakeProfitsEasy

Table of Contents

- INTRODUCTION 5
- CHAPTER I: STRATEGY I - COMMAND YOURSELF . 12
  - CONQUERING FEAR & EGO 14
  - CONQUERING FAILURE 22
  - CONQUERING LAZINESS 25
  - ACCEPTING THE MOMENT 28
- CHAPTER 2: STRATEGY 2 - CONTROL YOUR TROOPS 31
  - ORGANIZATION AND MORALE 33
  - RALLYING CRY: ON MOTIVATION 37
  - USING PEOPLE'S ABILITY: BATTLE FORMATIONS 42
- CHAPTER 3: STRATEGY 3 – METHODS OF ATTACK 48
  - BRUTE STRENGTH: THE DIRECT ATTACK ... 51
  - GUERILLA WARFARE 59
  - ON RETREAT AND PATIENCE 70
- CHAPTER 4: STRATEGY 4 – PSYCHOLOGICAL WARFARE 77
  - SHAPING THE BATTLEFIELD 77
  - THE ART OF PERSUASION 82
- CHAPTER 5: TYING IT ALL TOGETHER 87
  - USING ALL THE STRATEGIES 92
- CHAPTER 6: Coaching and FURTHER READING 98

INTRODUCTION

The world is changing; as globalization sweeps the planet, and the world economy struggles, competition has become fiercer. The number of people gunning for your job, clients and work are far greater than in the past. You need a new framework for fending off these individuals.

And, for that, we look to the past: to the timeless strategies of military masters such as Attila the Hun, Hannibal of Carthage, Sun Tzu, Genghis Khan, Miyamoto Musashi and more. Business, much like war, is a cutthroat, kill-or-be-killed endeavor. If you are not constantly on guard and aware of your competitors' moves, they will crush you before you can even blink.

Crushing the Competition is not only about how to defend yourself against your adversaries, but how to maneuver, outthink and ultimately defeat them. *Crushing the Competition* draws upon other classic military texts, such as *The Art of War* and *The Book of Five Rings*; business, like war, is almost boundless in what tactics an individual can employ. Strategies, however, are timeless; this book aims to illuminate the important ones, so that you may explore them further, and deeper, or simply note when your competitors attempt to use them against you. As Robert Greene writes in *The 33 Strategies of War,* strategy is about the macro view: your command of the entire operation. Tactics are about the current situation, choosing how to react or attack in the moment.

Without strategy, you cannot form tactics. Tactics change, are fluid; strategy is a mindset, a creed. Tactics always flow from strategy. Strategy leads you to your chief purpose—what you wish to accomplish with this specific battle. Without knowing your chief purpose, the end game, your tactics will be misguided, unorganized, poorly planned and worthless.

As Sun Tzu's seminal *The Art of War* states, "The Art of War teaches us to rely not on the likelihood of the enemy's not coming, but on our own readiness to receive him. Not on the chance of his not attacking, but on the fact that we have made our position unassailable."

Your enemies will come. They will be prepared. You must be more prepared. Your strategies must be sound; you must practice them, focus upon them, live them. Then you may, as Sun Tzu said many years ago, make your position unassailable. You will be ready for all contingencies. This short book contains four chief strategies, each outlined in a chapter with historical, as well as practical, examples.

The first, Command Yourself, is about the war within. You cannot be a great business leader without first controlling yourself. Becoming an excellent commander requires complete control over your mind, actions and emotions—for if you do not have dominion over yourself, how can you claim quarter over your enemies?

The second, Command Your Troops, is a primer on how to rally people to your cause. While you may be strong, and your ideas excellent, you cannot embark upon this journey alone. Even if you are an independent entrepreneur, it is inevitable that you will employ the services of others during your campaign. You must understand how to motivate, encourage and, if necessary, cut ties with your team.

The third strategic chapter is called Methods of Attack. This is an overview of various battle methodologies: the direct attack, guerilla warfare, and the power of retreat. Too often, we only have one method of attack for a problem because we are poorly versed in or unaware of other strategies. This will prove fatal for an entrepreneur, as the world presents an ever-changing array of challenges. Adapt, or you will meet an early demise.

The fourth, and final, chapter on strategy is titled Psychological Warfare. Our enemies often appear strong—in number, in available resources, in their market position—but they are weak emotionally, have insecurities. They have not learned how to command themselves or their troops, which leaves them susceptible to psychological attack and other mind games. Psychological warfare is perhaps the most effective, and most tricky, of all strategies to successfully employ. It requires tremendous discipline, and an intimate knowledge of your competitor, as well as mastery of the previously outlined strategies, to be effective.

Then we'll tie all these together. The great strategist does not rely on a single strategy, no matter how effective it has proven in the past. He is always willing to attempt new things as the battlefield changes. He never allows a strategy to become a crutch, nor is he reticent to fill holes within his knowledge. The truly successful entrepreneur is always learning, always attempting to grow; for he knows if he does not, then the world will leave him behind.

The main purpose of this text is to ensure that doesn't happen. It is time to claim your place at the forefront of the battlefield. Let's begin.

CHAPTER I: STRATEGY I - COMMAND YOURSELF

Modern life is full of distractions: email, cell phones, streaming television and other advances have made our world one full of stimuli. As an entrepreneur, you will have many different people, tasks and distractions vying for your time. Some of these appear under the guise of urgency, such as phone calls from your partners, others veil themselves as important, such as emails or other busy-work.

Before you can command the battlefield, before you can conquer the competition, before you can garner the respect of your peers and employees, you must be able to control yourself. This is not as easy as it first sounds. In fact, it will be the most challenging part of your campaign. We have been conditioned by modern life to be helpless, to succumb to the sirens' call of temptation far too easily.

We are bombarded with advertisements—10,000 a day, by some estimates—and other desires. Our dreams of success can cloud our vision, making us count our earnings, wealth and fame before they appear. And then, just as quickly as those visions appear, they will vanish, like clouds on the horizon.

Distraction comes in many forms. Your task, then, is to become a little more resilient to it each day. This is not easy, nor will you ever be in complete command of your being. But, in a legion of short attention spans, it will certainly appear that way. And your competition will cower in fear at your mighty abilities.

Some call this discipline. Others call it willpower, focus.

Whatever term you wish to apply, know that success in any endeavor—military or otherwise—first comes from within.

CONQUERING FEAR & EGO

We are all afraid. We are afraid when we are born, fighting for our first breath before breaking into a deluge of sobs. We are afraid on our death beds, as life slowly slips through our grasp. Fear is a normal emotion. It is a good emotion—it has kept us alive for many millennia, safe from the animals, people and plagues that wish us harm.

But it is easy to become a slave to fear, particularly in this modern world, where many concerns have been eradicated. Despite this book's focus on war, for example, it is unlikely that your home front has been directly touched by its shadowy pall. It is unlikely you have gone hungry; it is unlikely that wild animals threaten your existence.

If you have experienced such things, then you are one step ahead of the rest of us. You have tasted true fear, which makes it far easier to identify—and short-circuit—our fake fears.

These fake fears are usually born of ego: what if my business fails? What if I go broke? What if people don't like my product? What if people don't like *me*? We have all considered these questions many times. It is doubtful that any of these disastrous scenarios came to pass.

And, if they did—if someone did not like your product—you are still reading this. You did not die of embarrassment, nor was your career ruined. There were no (or very few) consequences; in fact, if you have failed, then you learned something. You are further ahead of your competition.

But your ego cannot accept that. Your ego is scared.

Great commanders in history—Attila the Hun, Genghis Khan, Sun Tzu—were thought to have tremendous egos. Historians have painted them as legends, military geniuses who were superior to their adversaries in every way. Bowed down to by mere mortals.

And they were legends, of sorts, but it took years of practice to achieve this. *Years*. They were not smiled upon by the Gods, or by talent; they were driven to outwork their competition. Their hands were mortal, just as yours are. Where their enemies put ten hours into planning an attack, they put in a hundred, drew maps and wrote stratagems until their bones grew weary. And then they kept going.

Their decisions were not born of ego, but of confidence. While it is certain that these men had egos—we all do—their confidence, training and knowledge dictated their decisions. Poor commanders make decisions based upon fear; excellent commanders make decisions from absolute knowledge.

They have complete focus.

Take Napoleon, one of history's greatest generals. This man's ego was unsurpassed by almost anyone in history, giving birth to the term "Napoleon complex." But, early in his career, his successes were not born of this irascible ego. He may have coveted greatness, but his singular focus was always on victory. He planned incessantly, rarely sleeping. This focus on the battle allowed his ego no quarter; the facts were laid out before him, in the maps of Europe, in the position of his and his opponents' armies. There was no room to think about the greatness that would ensue from victory. He had to plan for every contingency, every possible reaction from his enemy.

This was all that mattered, and Napoleon quickly became Emperor of France as a result.

Unfortunately, once he ascended to the throne, his focus turned from winning battles to building an empire. He wished to rule all of Europe, conquer Russia.

Napoleon the General surely knew this was foolhardy; his advisors told him as such, repeatedly. But Napoleon the Emperor was focused on glory, already counting his wealth, fame and land holdings. He deployed an army of over 450,000 men in June 1812, sending them to Russia.

He had not planned, however, for the fight that the Russians would put up when defending their homeland. They burned their fields, burned foodstuffs, and burned towns and cities—depriving Napoleon's army of supplies.

The harsh Russian winter began to set in. Napoleon lost more troops to starvation and sickness than to the Russian force—which his original army could have easily crushed, had they not kept retreating.

By November 1812, less than six months after invading Russia, Napoleon had less than 40,000 troops. The grandest army in the world had been defeated by a ragtag Russian force. Napoleon attempted to regroup his troops and bolster their numbers, but the battle was already lost. He died in exile.

In the past, when his focus was on winning the battle, he would have no doubt understood the Russian's intense love of their country. He would have planned for better supply lines, timed the campaign better to avoid the brutal winter.

But his focus was on riches, of how history would remember his grand victory. The ego is lazy; his being no exception, he believed that he could crush the Russians with a massive force, with superior resources. He was afraid that history would not remember him. He was afraid that people did not respect him—he was not royal, had ascended to the throne via military might rather than his blood.

History, in its eventuality, will remember none of us. We will all be swept into dust at one point. There is nothing to fear. When fear comes, we must simply accept that it is irrational. Unless there is an immediate danger, there is no reason to be fearful. It will cause you to rush, plan poorly or do less than ethical things.

Push your comfort zone a little bit every day. Do something that makes you feel uncomfortable. This is how fear dies: by pushing against the boundaries of your cell, teaching yourself that the world isn't scary. Do not allow your ego to tell you otherwise, allow you to sit upon your laurels, bask in past successes.

If you do not keep pushing, you will eventually fail. Fear never dies; all that we can hope, then, is to face and defeat it, every day.

CONQUERING FAILURE

No one likes failing. It brings back bad memories of school, where we didn't study for a test, or the teacher thought we were dumb because we got a 50 on a math exam.

Teachers don't tell you, however, that failure is essential in life. That, really, the only failure is a lack of effort. Not trying is the only failure that exists.

So show up.

In the above example, Napoleon failed because he didn't put in the effort. He stopped planning. He stopped thinking. His mind grew lazy.

You cannot fail if you put in the effort. No matter what—even if your product flops, your employees hate you, and your company crashes and burns. Because you will have learned so much—about life and about business—that such an experience cannot be seen as a failure.

You will understand, intimately, how to correct your mistakes next time.

The dirty secret about entrepreneurship is that the first time around, you usually fail. And the second time and the third time. Why? Because the competition is *fierce*. Being an entrepreneur is a great gig—and don't ever forget that, even in the midst of turmoil or 14 hour work days—and people are willing to bleed for a shot at freedom.

You have a lot of smart, dedicated people gunning for you. And it takes experience, trial by fire, to figure out how to survive. This is not failure; this is part of the process.

If you give up, then you have failed. This does not mean you can't shelve a project; if a project is terrible, or your product is awful, or your company is failing, then step away. Retreat and regroup. But come up with another idea—another hundred ideas—while you do this. Don't quit on being an entrepreneur. Some ideas don't work. You just can't quit on yourself.

That cannot happen. You must always try. Trying means executing your ideas as best you can. Sometimes that's not good enough. But that is part of being an entrepreneur. Keep executing and you will succeed. Never execute and you will fail.

It's that simple: do more.

CONQUERING LAZINESS

There is no way around this: to succeed as an entrepreneur, you will have to put in the time. A lot of time. More than your 9 – 5. More than you did in college. More than you've ever put in during your entire life.

You will fight this, and you will not accept it at first. Your brain will revolt. You became an entrepreneur to break free of the system—but you'll find, at least in the beginning, that the truth is not so rosy. Your responsibilities will grow ten-fold. There will be no boss to get things done; you are the boss. You will not get paid unless you work, unlike at your 9 – 5, where you could sneak off and play *Farmville* on the company's dime.

You must learn what tasks are important, demand your time, what can be delegated, and what simply should be ignored.

This is a process; the great generals were not born disciplined. They had a vision, and slowly their skills and dedication grew to fit their grandiose dreams. This took time, however; discipline is a skill. It must be exercised, just like your muscles, otherwise it will atrophy and you will become lazy.

The simplest defense against laziness is to do work that you want to do. It sounds flippant, telling you to find your passion, but this is the best way to ensure that work gets done. Even when you're passionate about a project, you will still have lulls. But you will be able to break through them, because you can see what's on the other side.

Sun Tzu was intensely passionate about war, about defending his homeland from invaders. He was willing to die, plan, strategize at all hours of the day to achieve this goal. His loyalty and sense of honor drove him to greatness. If you are not willing to die for your product or business, then you might be in the wrong field.

If you are still tempted to play *Farmville* instead of unleashing your entrepreneurial venture on the world, you must try something different. If you lack ideas, read. Read great books, read blogs, read everything that you can acquire.

Ideas will surge, and you will find something that sings to you.

Discipline can be built. This process is necessary. But the surest path to success and crushing the competition is through passion. This cannot be replicated. You will outwork others not because you are grinding, but because of enjoyment, of dedication. Work born of dedication and belief will always have an intense focus that the competition cannot match.

ACCEPTING THE MOMENT

Entrepreneurs are driven. They have to be; competition dictates as such. If you are not driven, then you will not succeed—someone else is always nipping at your heels, waiting for you to become lazy or passive.

Being driven, however, can be a negative. In fact, it often leads to fear, failure and laziness. This is simply because, as an entrepreneur, the vision you hold within your mind is often far from your current reality. You want to change the world, perhaps, but right now you might be working out of your garage, on the first product prototype.

Every great general in history learned to accept circumstances for how they currently were. It was no good to wish for more troops, different terrain, a smaller enemy force, or better weapons. The current situation was all that existed; their strategies and tactics, thus, had to flow from reality, not from wishes or impossible desires.

Likewise, you must accept your current situation, work from within the moment. If you stare off too far in the future, you will lose your way; if you lament mistakes or stumbles in the past, you will be too distracted. Work intensely within the moment, and accept that this, right now, is where you must be.

You could be nowhere else; your decisions have led you here. Embrace the present. It is the only reality that exists. Realize what you must do to get where you are headed, then use your current time to achieve it.

CHAPTER 2: STRATEGY 2 - CONTROL YOUR TROOPS

Respect is born of confidence. Your employees, freelancers and other individuals you come across will not respect when you are undeserving of it. You may hide behind a mask of false confidence, but savvy people—the type that will enhance your organization, prove useful allies—will easily see through this.

Thus, the first step lies in the previous chapter: command yourself. Work on yourself, each and every day. When you have achieved confidence, knowledge and attained skills, you may be tempted to taper off, coast. This is when you must redouble your efforts. The stakes are high if you do not; all the time you invested in yourself could, ultimately, be for naught.

Books like *The Law of Attraction* and self-help blogs suggest that if you desire something, then it will become true. That if you are successful, successful people will flock to you. This is a nice platitude, but it is just that: comforting words that do not hold a place within the walls of reality.

The truth is this: the universe does not care about you. It holds no stock in your success. People owe you nothing. They do not care about your success, either—only how it pertains to their own. This is harsh, but it is best to see the world as it is, rather than through rose-tinted lenses. The latter will make blood appear indistinguishable from water.

They are not the same.

People, however, will not sabotage or work against you if they respect you. This is tricky to accomplish, of course, but like all good things in life—and business—it is a worthwhile undertaking.

ORGANIZATION AND MORALE

Many bosses rule with an iron fist. They berate their employees, controlling them through intimidation, fear-mongering and veiled threats. This iron fist can be direct, or it can be more subtle—the latter is much more common. If you do not show up for work, for example, you will be fired. Thus, you show up, for fear of losing your job.

They believe this is effective, for it has been the accepted way of doing things for years.

But isn't it better for your employees to show up not out of fear, but love? For them to work every day not because they have to, but because they want to? This sounds like a utopian ideal, particularly for a book called *Crushing the Competition*. But, in order to beat the competition, you must first take care of your own house. The bloodiest wars are often not fought between bitter adversaries, but between those once considered allies. If you can avoid fighting with your employees and rally them to your cause, then you are already far ahead of your competitors. A unified force can never be thwarted by a disorganized opponent.

The chief rule is to lead by example. If you expect your employees to work hard, you must first prove that you are willing to do so. Respect is earned; while money can contract mercenaries, vision and execution are the currency with which you purchase true allies. You must actively include your employees in your decisions, make them feel that their opinions, ideas and personalities are valued.

The corporate world is often soul-crushing; it involves taking cheap labor to make CEOs and other higher-ups millions. A man's individuality is not cherished; in fact, it is a negative—it disrupts the assembly line, throws a wrench in the flow of the proceedings. Corporations want automatons, and, indeed, it should come as no surprise that many jobs have subsequently been robotized or otherwise automated over the past twenty years. This trend is likely to continue, as modernity's incessant march continues forward.

This provides an opening for the astute commander; instead of treating your workers as generators or commodities, you must consider them to be people. Perhaps this sounds rudimentary, but the most fundamental and important tenets of war—and business—are all simple. Their application can prove difficult, particularly in a noisy and distracting world, but the concepts are easy enough for a child to grasp.

Thus, to repeat: treat your employees with respect. Listen to their concerns. This does not mean you must take action upon their concerns, or entertain all ideas. Many ideas and notions are bad or detrimental. As the leader, it is your job to discern excellent ideas from the multitude of mediocre ones. But you should always listen, keeping your ear to the ground for rumblings, concerns and what's on your organization's mind.

And, above all else, lead by example. If you're lazy, party all day or are otherwise disengaged from your work, how can you expect your employees to pick up the slack? As Sun Tzu wrote, "Enact consistency in orders and instruction and the men will be loyal to you; if there is no consistency, they will not."

Consistency begins in your own house, with the cultivation of control over yourself. Do what you must, and so will the people under your command. Don't, and you shall be torn apart.

RALLYING CRY: ON MOTIVATION

People crave purpose in their lives; they want their lives to have meaning. Most corporate jobs are the anti-thesis of this ideal; they extract people's skills and work, leaving nothing in return. The employee never sees the fruits of their labor; it is simply lost in a nebulous, swirling current.

If you can rally your employees to your cause, their work and energy will soar. Your competition will not stand a chance.

An easy solution to this is to hire like-minded people—those passionate about your realm of expertise and the direction of the company. Another is to have a customer or people oriented focus; employees of non-profits, for example, are often motivated not by pay, but the work they're doing.

This, of course, might not be realistic, depending on your organizational structure and the focus of your company. That's okay—because there are other ways to encourage your employees and get them to do their best work.

In short, your focus should be to create a focused culture. This might require a mission statement, or a clear company mantra. It might simply diffuse naturally, spreading throughout the company organically. But your employees must know what they are working for.

They must have a clear, vibrant purpose.

Hannibal of Carthage was a master of engendering purpose in the Carthaginian troops. Unlike many other great commanders, there are no historical records of mutiny or revolt from within his ranks; his men were wholly committed to his campaigns and vision. This is no small feat, considering that Hannibal lead them through the Alps in 218 BC; this unconventional method of attack, which by some accounts *halved* his troop total, caught the Romans off-guard and changed the landscape of the Roman empire for the next fifteen years.

By being a master tactician and negotiator, Hannibal managed to convince some of the Gaul tribes that he met in the frigid mountains to either join him or allow him to pass through the native-controlled regions. This was no doubt a product of his concise vision: to defeat the Romans and spread the glory of Carthage.

A simple goal, no doubt, as most people carry some form of patriotism and national pride within their breasts—particularly when they are the object of another power's oppression.

The Romans were, at the time, the most powerful presence in the ancient world. Their reach extended from Europe to Asia to Africa; indeed, an empire of this scope has not been seen since. The Carthaginians were defeated by the Romans in the First Punic War of 264 – 241 BC (Hannibal was born in 247 BC), after which the Romans levied some rather strict military and economic sanctions upon Carthage. Carthage's magnificent navy was heavily reduced, and they were forced to pay an indemnity of 2,200 talents of silver, plus 1,000 talents annually. In modern terms, the former penalty amounted to 66 tons.

Rome had the most feared army and military presence in the world. Her reach spanned almost the entire known globe. Most men would cower in fear in her shadow, but Hannibal's boldness and deft tactics spurred his army into believing, rallying about him. It was said, many years after Hannibal's ultimate defeat and demise, Roman

Senators, in the face of disaster, would whisper *Hannibal ad portas* (Hannibal is at the gates). Indeed, this man from Carthage, shortly after emerging from the Alps, met the legendary Roman force at the Battle of Trebia with only 40,000 troops—many of which had been recently enlisted from the tribes of Gaul.

And won, shattering them with unconventional tactics and an intense army unmatched by even the legendary Roman Legionaries.

USING PEOPLE'S ABILITY: BATTLE FORMATIONS

A great strategist plays to his army's strengths. If his force is comprised of archers, he finds high ground from whence they can rain arrows down upon the enemy; if he finds strength in his cavalry, he will search out terrain that will benefit their speed and flanking ability.

Similarly, an excellent entrepreneur understands his company's strengths and weaknesses, and has an intimate knowledge of his employees' capabilities. It is important to find individuals with skills; there are many with credentials, pieces of paper and other frivolous accolades that translate poorly to the fires of the real world. Find those who can execute well—regardless of their prior resume—and you will serve your company well.

That being said, it is not enough to find those with skills. Even the best equipped and trained army will fall to a motley foe if the commander throws them into battle with little heed of their strengths. He must grant them autonomy, trust them to fight valiantly against the enemy. Similarly, the commander delegates much of his responsibility to generals, lieutenants, sergeants and other field commanders. He understands and trusts his team to execute his plan and march towards their shared vision; he also understands that it is impossible for him to be at all places at once.

Battle formations, at least when viewed through an entrepreneurial lens, amount to your ability to correctly delegate. Artists should work on your company's graphics; this much is clear. But certain artists are better equipped for web design, others for logo work, still others for creating promotional material like brochures. *Look* at an individual's cadre of skills, not just her title or degree. It is quite possible that, while appearing as an artist in title, she also carries marketing acumen or significant writing ability within her as well. This extra ability is wasted if you merely have her drawing logos—she is better suited to creating beautiful marketing spreads and ad campaigns.

Find these latent abilities and use them to attack a problem with efficiency and ingenuity. In the above scenario, you might even save money; if your artist is an excellent copywriter, you can roll two jobs into one. As any commander knows, conserving resources and soldiers is key to victory; if you can use one team member instead of two, then that is a significant strategic win.

Delegation also requires humility. Many CEOs, presidents and leaders fret over delegation because they crave absolute control. They wish for a problem to be attacked *their* way, and only in this fashion. They do not trust their teams.

This is toxic; if you do not trust your team, then they will not trust you either. The relationship will be reciprocal, and distrust will breed throughout your organization. Whether dealing with employees or freelancers, you must trust in the person's ability to execute your vision. You must also acknowledge that your vision, once shared with another, becomes collective. Your themes, your ideas, they may still dominate the field of view—but it will no longer solely be yours once you place a job in another's hands.

This might sound worrisome, or even nausea inducing, but this is not the case; in fact, this is a blessing, a way to further leverage abilities in your team that you might have missed. If you have assembled a team of talented individuals, their ideas will no doubt be valid—some will even be good, providing perspective on the problem that you lack. No matter how good a commander you prove to be, there will always be a method, a tactic, an approach that escapes your own thoughts. This is why we work with others: to find those things that we missed.

Trust in the skills of others. Play to their strengths, and grant them autonomy to tackle problems on their own. You cannot command the entire battle; you must set the plan, set the tone, then allow your people to execute the strategy and react to the throes of war. The world is fluid, fast and moving faster every day; there is not enough time for you to micromanage.

Focus on execution and you will swiftly fell new problems, outpacing your competition.

CHAPTER 3: STRATEGY 3 – METHODS OF ATTACK

The ways in which you can confront your opponent are almost innumerable; tactics, nuances and situation-dependent methods, thus, are too vast to enumerate here. Thus, we will focus upon three methods of attack that have proven popular and ubiquitous through the centuries.

The first is one of brute strength: the direct charge, whence you attack your opponent's forces head on, in a clear-cut struggle of strength. Little strategy or tactics; just an all-out assault wherein the stronger force wins the day.

The second is guerilla warfare, which has risen in popularity in recent decades. This involves fighting in the shadows, from rooftops and trees, hitting the enemy with surprise before disappearing into the terrain. Quick, mobile and low-cost, this type of attack is difficult to plan for, because by its very nature it is spontaneous (although it is often well-planned and quite strategic; it only appears sudden to the foe under fire) and unexpected.

The third and final method of attack might not seem like an aggressive maneuver at all: it is the power of retreat, of patience. Many great commanders used retreats—both feigned and real—to set their opponents up for a fall. Although on the surface this is a defensive maneuver, the power of retreat recalls the old adage *the best offense is a good defense*. In many situations, retreat and patience will open up an enemy for mistakes—making it a sneaky and effective method of aggression.

All of these methods can—and will—be used in tandem to lead your company to victory. Their use depends on the situation at hand, your available resources and, of course, the strength of your competition. There is no one-size-fits-all prescription for battle stratagems; as Sun Tzu writes in *The Art of War,* "There are no constants in warfare, any more than water maintains a constant shape."

May you be like water, then, possessing the requisite knowledge to react to any problem that arises on your entrepreneurial journey.

BRUTE STRENGTH: THE DIRECT ATTACK

A common misconception of the neophyte entrepreneur is that they need more: more capital, more employees, more skills, more contacts. This is often responsible for people's reluctance to start a business at all.

They think that victory is always won through brute force, rather than strategy. The only method of attack that they hold within their minds is the direct clash, where they throw their collected resources against a problem. And, in the end, either it yields, or they do.

This is ridiculous and ineffective. The direct attack, as with other attack strategies, has its moments. But to rely on it as the core of your battle strategy is foolhardy. Even if your resources are vast, you will incur wasteful losses and degrade your troop's morale. You can only incur so many losses and costs in a given campaign before your coffers are exhausted and the battle is lost. Recall Napoleon's ill-fated invasion of Russia; he thought that his superior force and resources would see his victory through. The might and glory of France far exceeded that of lowly Russia; in fact, Russia was only of interest because of its vast array of natural resources, its positioning and what it could do for the French Empire. Its people, their spirit and their resolve played little into Napoleon's calculations; he thought this troops would roll over this desolate wasteland, crush the opposition, and gain an easy victory.

Instead, he lost more than 300,000 troops, and ultimately his throne.

However, an effective example of a direct attack can be found at the Battle of Thermopylae. Fictionalized in the movie *300*, King Leonidas of Sparta faced off against the Persian Empire, led by Xerxes I for over three days in 480 BC. The catch, of course, was that Sparta had but five thousand men (the Spartans totaled 300, but they had a little help—though not much—from their Thespian and Theban allies). Xerxes, though myths tell of a million strong force, had an army of over 100,000 troops.

The smaller force had but one advantage; they held the pass at Thermopylae, which did not allow Xerxes' army to spread out and enjoy its superior force through numbers. In fact, the pass was nearly impregnable. Xerxes launched a number of frontal assaults on the pass, coupled with arrow fire (that was defended against by the bronze helmets and shields of the Greeks). Despite his superior numbers, these attacks failed—even when Xerxes sent his elite troops, dubbed the Immortals, to capture the pass and the pernicious Greeks. Eventually, Xerxes decided that flanking the set-in Greeks would be the only way to defeat them. Upon this occurring, Leonidas insisted that the troops other than the 300 Spartans leave and flee. About 3,000 left, leaving a force of perhaps 1,500 to go up against the Persians.

On the 3rd day of battle, these troops were finally defeated, every last one of them dying—but not before Xerxes lost 20,000 men in his direct assault. This might seem an egregious number, and indeed, direct assaults are often costly—but Xerxes' force was large enough that this proved a relatively negligible loss. In fact, the pass should have been held longer—by combining the direct attack with flanking maneuvers, Xerxes flushed the Greeks out, scoring a victory. Although some accounts suggest that his attack led to his defeat some months later, this is hardly the case. In fact, it was an ill-planned retreat that did him in—his fear dictated his later actions, where he was terrified of being trapped in Greece (the Greeks were blocking various trails and bridges, and Xerxes' navy had been largely eradicated).

The majority of his troops died of exhaustion, starvation and disease when fleeing back to Persia. The next year, the Greeks ended the Persian invasion at the Battle of Plataea, despite Xerxes mustering up a renewed force. This series of events, however, was not because of his direct attack at Thermopylae; rather, it was because he lacked command of himself, his own fear—weaknesses which were later brought out by clever Grecian tactics. Foreshadowing of this psychological weakness could be seen following the aftermath at Thermopylae: Xerxes ordered Leonidas' body to be beheaded and crucified, an egregious act of disrespect born of temper, rather than reason. This infuriated the Greeks when they heard of how their brave general's corpse had been desecrated; later, they used this knowledge to engage in unconventional tactics.

When does the direct attack have value? When a problem is small, or when your enemies are scattered or weak. When you have significant numbers, it is best to attack the problem, even if it is costly. If Xerxes had waited, he never would have made it through the pass; the Greeks would have bolstered their troops eventually, making passage all but impossible.

It is ineffectual to deliberate and strategize for every minor issue that crops up—these must be addressed and squashed quickly, preferably by your team. When your competition is unsure, mutinying, small in stature or on the ropes, this is the time to hammer home your own superiority and bravely charge forth. This might mean releasing new products or battening down the hatches and working at all hours to get new features ready. It might mean trying to acquire them, or grab some of their best talent.

Or, if you're working on your own, it could simply mean seizing opportunity amidst a paradigm shift. For example, if you were an author around 2007 or 2008 with a decent fan base, you would have done well for your career to start independently publishing—the traditional publishers were reeling with the release of Amazon's Kindle, totally unsure how to react to the new landscape.

Those who charged bravely ahead, though they might not have had a solid strategy—or absolute knowledge of the battlefield—were rewarded for their bravery. There was confusion amongst the ranks, and a scattering of opinions; some believed the Kindle would fail, others believed it would lead to a publishing revolution (which, in fact, is what occurred). Where others are meek, you should be strong; but in any direct attack, you must not leave your flank or rear exposed. Never commit all of your resources to one offensive, for it is possible that the new paradigm fades, and the old one regains its dominance. Betting the house eventually always leads to ruin.

Be prepared for both scenarios, exposing yourself to as much opportunity and good fortune as you can. But do so quickly, for these opportunities soon vanish—seized by the boldest of others.

GUERILLA WARFARE

Guerilla warfare might suggest less than noble means of engaging the enemy—terrorism, for one, comes to mind. And while terrorism is a subset of guerilla warfare, the general theme of this strategy is not about fighting dirty. Rather, it is about bootstrapping what resources you have together in order to form innovative and new tactics. Guerilla warfare is about using your perceived disadvantages—a smaller force, less training—to form advantages against larger, less nimble opponents.

In the business world, monolithic corporations have ingrained cultures and methods of doing things. These have proven effective in the past, but the future is uncertain, ever-changing; one day, perhaps today, these methods will prove fallacious, outdated. If you're a start-up or a small player, you have no such loyalties to outdated methodologies; you do not have customers who expect things to be done a certain way, even if that approach is inefficient.

As such, you are free to chart your own strategy, one that fits your organization's strengths and uses its weaknesses in unique ways.

Guerilla warfare, in many ways, is the direct opposite of brute strength. It requires cunning, planning and intense attention to detail. Whereas resources are often squandered in a frontal assault, no resources can be lost in a guerilla attack—each one is precious, and must be conserved. You must receive maximum returns for minimal expenditures: this is the tenet at the heart of all guerilla warfare campaigns.

In modern times, companies have done this by leveraging the power of the internet—galvanizing large customer bases through blogging, social media and other recent innovations. Sometimes referred to as "guerilla marketing," this is the antithesis of traditional marketing, the zenith of which is advertising during primetime television to the tune of hundreds of thousands of dollars.

These campaigns, by contrast, sometimes cost nothing—with the exception of time—and can have enormous returns. Another recent innovation includes street teams—popular for artists, who encourage their fans to give out freebies, hang posters and push their work across the country. Of course, guerilla warfare in the entrepreneurial sense is hardly limited to marketing; it spans all aspects of your business, and is as much cultural as it is a strategy.

It is a way of life, a value system that pits *you* against *them*—typically in a prototypical David and Goliath showdown. This is an essential part of your identity, and it's something that your fans and employees connect with. It is about the hustle, the grind and being able to bootstrap your way to success. Guerilla warfare commanders don't have posh NYC offices; that is the domain of larger foes.

In the annals of history, perhaps no group was more famous for their frightening guerilla tactics than the Huns. Under the rule of Attila—who was dubbed the Scourge of God by his foes—the Huns terrorized the Roman Empire from 434 – 453 AD, when Attila died.

The Huns were Eurasian nomads from the rocky steppes. It is unclear where they originated from, although their fearsome dedication to military tactics and facial features have drawn comparisons to Genghis Khan's similarly mobile Mongol Horde, some centuries later. Wherever they emerged from, their battle prowess was admirable, and the Romans, by the early 5th

century, had their hands full from the nomadic cavalry.

Their lack of a homeland (though they did have the makings of an empire at the time of Attila's death) made the Huns liable to show up at any moment, sacking whatever villages and cities they chose. And, indeed, Attila led them on many campaigns: against the Rhine, to Constantinople, and even to Rome. Though he failed to wrest control of any of these locales permanently from the Romans, the once-mighty empire lived in constant fear of Attila's attacks. Although the Huns negotiated various peace treaties with the Romans, these were often dishonored at a moment's notice, whenever their bloodlust saw fit. Their mounted archers were formidable and fleet opponents, with some who met them in battle claiming them to be invincible.

Their mobility granted them a host of tactics unavailable to conventional armies comprised mainly of infantry. Perhaps the most unusual was Attila's willingness to retreat and head back to the Hungarian Plains, even when more land and cities were available for conquest. No better example of this lies than in his assault of Northern Italy in 452 AD. Pressing onwards, with a victory against Venice, Attila suddenly stopped, turning around. As Italy had suffered from terrible famine during the previous two years, Attila concluded that a sacking of Rome would be of little benefit.

Due to his nomadic origins, he was unshackled by the notion of traditional empire building, in which oft-worthless land holdings and cities were rolled under one's command merely for the sake of empty glory. Instead of capturing Rome, which had little in the ways of supplies due to the famine—and certainly not enough to sustain his army—Attila accepted peace and returned to the Great Hungarian Plains. Although he died the following year, his decision—though unconventional, and perhaps not an "attack" in the literal sense of the word—was a brilliant tactical move, and the essence of guerilla warfare.

You must be uninhibited by traditional modes of thinking—there will be many who tell you what is right, or the way things must be done. Capturing Rome for the sake of it might have been a "victory" for Attila, but it would do little to enhance the well-being of his people or strengthen his army's position. As such, he eschewed riding onwards, even when the city lay within his grasp.

This would seem foolhardy to many commanders, who would be swept up in grandiose visions of sacking the city and realizing control over the centuries-old capital of the ancient world. But Attila realized that a paradigm shift had occurred; Rome was no longer the fair maiden of former years, and held little value.

The guerilla entrepreneur will not see many awards, accolades or pats on the back. In fact, the establishment will fight your every action—that is why you must be subversive, striking quickly from the shadows of the forest before retreating back, away from the skirmish. You do not have to be bloodthirsty or brutal, as the Huns used to be; instead be pragmatic, intelligent, and realize that your small position is actually a blessing. You can be nimble where others cannot; your inexperience allows you to try new things without worry of failure.

Consider the plight of the Americans against the British during the Revolutionary War. The British, though far better trained, armed and staffed, succumbed to what essentially amounted to a militia. Part of the reason was belief, the morale: the Americans were fighting for their homeland, and they had a purpose. But the real reason was that the British were caught in old modes of thinking, wherein factions met "honorably" on the field of battle, in a direct assault.

There is little honor in war. It is brutal, unforgiving; the British mistakenly thought they could tame this domain of murder and animalistic passion. They marched through forests in their beautiful red coats, only to be harassed and picked off by Americans lying in the bushes and hiding in the trees.

The British considered this not to be gentlemanly, but this is simply the excuse of a dying old guard. In business, some will say that the "kids" do not have any respect for the way things are done, the way things used to be.

All that you must respect is the work. Plan your attack, strategize and react according to what you see, not what you wish to see. Do this, and you will emerge victorious over the stodgy strategists and old-school monoliths who refuse to adjust to modern times. There is nothing dirty about this; in business, just as war, the rules are there merely for show.

We are all animals and opportunists. Forget that, and your competition will soon remind you of this harsh reality.

ON RETREAT AND PATIENCE

This book has mentioned a couple retreats—those of Napoleon and Xerxes—that ended in disaster. This might suggest that retreating is foolhardy; that notion, however, is incorrect. Retreating after the disaster has hit, and it is too late, will yield few benefits. You must identify when the tide is about to return, then remove your resources before the proverbial bomb drops.

It does little to remove your troops after the missile hits. You must do so beforehand, anticipating your opponent's moves. In business, your opponent is two-fold: both your competitors and the overall macroeconomic environment of your marketplace.

You must be intimately aware of the actions of your competitors, but, more importantly, you must be looking for trends in the entire fabric of your industry.

In battle, retreat really means regrouping and living to fight another day. It is not about cowardice, but about prudence. A mutinous flight—what happens during a rout—is not a retreat. This panicked maneuver will result in massive casualties. A retreat is a calculated strategic decision that places your army in a better position to emerge victorious in the future.

In business, this might involve backing off from a project that is siphoning resources and becoming a drag on the team. Whatever costs have been invested in the project are now sunk; throwing good money and time after bad is a recipe for failure. There are many business books that will tell you never to quit—that the only way you fail is to quit.

This is incorrect; you can fail if you do not recognize that a project is doomed or ineffective. It is important to maintain a critical, objective eye, and identify sticking points—even if this means taking a step back from your original vision. When you retreat, you have time to think and consider other options. By withdrawing, your thoughts are no longer engaged with the project, obsessed with it; you are free to think of alternatives or solutions to your current predicament.

Never be afraid *not* to finish; you can come back later, with a renewed force, and conquer the problem then.

Retreat is a product of patience. This is a world in which instant results are too slow; we have become accustomed to an endless blitz of feedback, stimuli and results. Good ideas take time to play out, even if you tackle their execution with fervor and intensity. You cannot force them to take root or develop faster; they will do so at their own pace, provided you have invested an ample amount of work in fostering their growth.

Most mistakes are born of impatience; this can lead to foolish wastes of resources, imprudent decisions and ruin. Patience is a skill, and it must be cultivated. There is a common Zen saying: when you don't have time to meditate for one hour, you must do so for two.

You are no doubt busy. Your free time is likely limited. This is when you must go slowest, be the most patient. Your mind cannot work and come up with ideas when you are distracted, constantly engaged. You must survey the battlefield, take time out of the day to assess your project's current state. Blindly moving forward in a blitz of work, while somewhat admirable, is often the wrong decision.

Patience will elevate you above all your competition. Almost no one has patience in this world; few ever did, even when a thousand things weren't vying for our attention. Your competitors may appear to be surpassing your efforts; this is an illusion. Patience builds a solid foundation, allows your business to grow at a sustainable pace. The tower will not outstrip the supports beneath it. You will not tackle problems before you are ready, before you have acquired the requisite skills to solve them.

When you find yourself most overwhelmed, take a step back. Do nothing—yes, nothing—for five, perhaps ten minutes. That means *nothing*; this is not a meditation, just a respite, a break from the action. Close your eyes, or don't, and simply exist. Focus on your breathing, taking deep breaths, if you prefer. When you return from this interlude, your mind will be freshened, and you will have additional ideas on how to deal with your struggles.

This will be difficult; more difficult than the 14 hour days and the endless deluge of work that seems to cascade upon your head like a waterfall. But it will pay the most dividends; this patience will soon wash over all your activities, and a calmness will permeate your existence that others will be in awe of.

CHAPTER 4: STRATEGY 4 – PSYCHOLOGICAL WARFARE

Honey is often more persuasive than vinegar. You can entrap your competitors, lull them to sleep without ever firing a shot; this requires great skill, but it is far less costly than the alternative. In many cases, psychological warfare begins from within: it is about controlling yourself and your troops, uniting them in a common goal.

SHAPING THE BATTLEFIELD

Psychological warfare is waged behind enemy lines, through newspapers, media and the power of ideas. In many ways, it is a battle of ideologies; whichever army's vision and dedication is stronger will win this form of battle. Without resolve or belief, their minds will crumble, and so will their ability to defend themselves against more conventional attacks.

To shape the battlefield, you must have a clear message. This requires a clarity of self and purpose; this can only come from you, the leader, and not from your employees. It must trickle down from your being, to those who answer to you. It cannot flow up; such is the nature of gravity. As Miyamoto Musashi writes in *The Book of 5 Rings,* "Such distortions are turning your back on the True Way. Know the meaning of this, and make straightforward your foundation. Make the heart of truth your Way, practice a broad spectrum of martial arts, and understand the expansive correctly and clearly."

What does he mean by the True Way? Simply, a clarity and intensity of purpose—an absolute dedication to your craft, your cause and your beliefs. You must possess these qualities before you can hope to sway the minds of others; people can sense lies and half-truths, even if they do not understand why they feel uneasy in your presence. This does not mean you must be radically honest—and, in fact, psychological warfare often deals in the currency of half-truths and insidious rumors—merely that you have presence and utmost belief in your actions.

Take, for instance, Hitler. While a terrible man, he was a master of propaganda, rallying the entirety of Germany against the world. If not for a few mistakes, it is conceivable that Hitler would have succeeded in accomplishing his twisted plan. But the real triumph was convincing the people of Germany that various ethnic groups were the cause of their pain. In truth, rather onerous war reparations from the first World War were the major culprit of Germany's economic woes—but Hitler inserted his own truth into the fold.

His message was clear, and possessed an intensity of focus that captivated the minds of the people. He utilized his message for great evil—and, indeed, other rulers, such as Mao, have used similar methods to tragic effect. They all shaped the battlefield, galvanizing their troops with a clear purpose. They framed the situation as they saw it, even if this was a distortion of reality. Their purpose, their words were uttered with such belief and ardent fervor that people couldn't help but follow.

Do not be discouraged, however; psychological warfare is not solely the domain of dictators and evil men. It is important to study all sides of warfare, so that you may understand what techniques your competition can use against you. You must understand how others frame their products, their platforms, so that you can use these tactics for better means. In the corporate world, companies use psychological appeals all the time—this is, in essence, what advertising is. They convince people to purchase things they do not need, with money they don't have, for happiness that will never come.

What, then, if you have something people *do* need? What if your service or offering can really change lives? That simply makes your job easier—you can use your purpose and clear message to convince people to follow you, instead of the competition. Good is always an easier sell than evil; inherently, we are drawn to it. Bear this in mind, even when it seems that your competitors or the world is intent on manipulation towards evil ends.

Be clear in your purpose. Understand it, live it. Then project it with intensity, find those who share your vision. Some may call this propaganda, others may call it advertising. But if your intentions are good and your message is sound, from the heart, then you will know it but by one name.

Truth.

THE ART OF PERSUASION

In short, you must provide value for others. This is how trust is formed, repeat business comes about, and your entrepreneurial venture grows. There are innumerable tricks and games that you can play with the people around you—the aforementioned propaganda, for instance—to get them on your side. However, these are often short-lived or temporary; tricks only work so far, and when the stakes are raised, people might question their dedication to your cause.

The only way to form relationships, the only way to truly persuade those around you to back your cause, is to provide them value. This can be in the form of information, skills, your product or service, or any other way you can help. But, before people will help you, you must help them. This forms a bond that is difficult to break; as humans, we want to reciprocate favors, support those who have supported us in the past.

There are exceptions to this rule, of course—sociopaths and bad people who will take, take,

take and give nothing in return. You will learn how to spot these individuals, and you will not repeat this mistake many times thereafter. But most people are decent, and will want to help those who have helped them in the past.

The best way to make a customer a repeat customer is to provide a valuable product. The best way to keep an excellent employee is to grant them praise for a job well done, grant them responsibilities that fit their skillset. The best way to find allies is to give them information, share with them your expertise—without strings or other considerations. Give, and you shall receive; this is the most persuasive of psychological tactics.

Why? Because it is genuine. In a world of bogus marketing gimmicks, you are the person who cuts through the clutter. Your honesty and willingness to help will be recognized instantly. It will be refreshing. Everyone is concerned with *the next big thing* or various gambits; if you are simply focused on providing value for all those around you, you will quickly persuade them to join your cause. It is not difficult to galvanize others when you expect nothing in return. They will follow and support you of their own accord.

The world is cutthroat, cruel and oftentimes demoralizing. The sweetness of honey—your honey—provides people a brief respite, a shroud from the harshness of reality. They will want to spend as much time underneath your shroud as possible—no cajoling or convincing necessary. This does not mean you must always be nice, or conciliatory, or a pushover; it simply means that you have skills and ideas that you are willing to share. You are generous where most are not. You have an abundance of wealth—and not necessarily in the traditional sense—that you share freely.

This is powerful, and people—good people, not evil-doers and grifters—will flock to this mentality. All you have to do is help them.

CHAPTER 5: TYING IT ALL TOGETHER

The master strategist does not rely upon a single tactic or strategy to emerge victorious. He combines the various techniques at his disposal to craft unique and unpredictable methods of attack that his opponent is unprepared for.

The inner game of war—that is, the mental component—far outstrips the physical in terms of importance. While it is vital that your army be trained, in shape and well-equipped, battles—particularly in the business world—are often won in the mind. This comes as a surprise to most, who believe that brute strength is how one crushes the competition. But, remember: every corporation was, at one point, just an upstart, scrappy and without major resources at their disposal.

It bears remembering that there is always someone better: bigger, smarter, with deeper pockets, more experience and so forth. This might sound depressing, but it actually provides you with significant opportunity: the ability to learn from your competition, scout out their weaknesses. This is your opportunity to craft a unique battle strategy, from the various pieces left to us from antiquity and modernity.

Going up against a superior opponent requires you to push yourself to greater heights. It forces your skills and thinking to evolve. An all-out assault takes little thought; a war of sedition, fought in the shadows, takes a great amount of tactical acumen, by contrast.

When squaring off against opponents—particularly those who could easily squash your venture—it is important to first understand yourself. Center your mind, your thoughts, place them solely on the task that will unfold before you. Nothing else exists; this is your focus, your new life. If you cannot dedicate yourself in such a fashion, then it is likely you are in the wrong industry, developing the wrong product, or are otherwise wasting your time.

Next, you must transfer this belief to those that surround you. It's possible that you're the lone person at your business; in this instance, make sure that your freelancers, suppliers or those who you interact with *feel* your energy and excitement. Transfer this to them, so that their work is born of the same intensity. Do not interact with others with a lukewarm demeanor; they will question your dedication, and they will question why they should invest a piece of themselves in the work they do for you. As such, it will be generic and forgettable. Allow them to see your undying love and passion for your enterprise; even if they are not interested in the concept, they will respect what you are trying to accomplish, and wish for their own work to reflect this same energy.

These tenets might seem Zen-esque, or otherwise spiritual in nature. But understand this: your mind and your body are your only possessions in this world. No matter how many businesses you start, no matter the number of dollars in your bank account, your existence begins and ends with your mind and body. War is about manipulating these two assets to greater effect and superior results than your opponent.

Business is the same. If your mind is weak, then your ideas will be weak, your actions will be weak and you will fail. You may temporarily grasp success, but it will quickly slip through your fingers. Thus, to build a sustainable enterprise, you must first work intensely upon yourself. There are a number of methods—some outlined in *Crushing the Competition*, others available via various quality books, blogs and mentors—through which you can achieve a solidarity of self.

But, before you can apply battle strategies or affect the external world with any degree of magnitude, you must become a strong person.

It is that simple; not easy, but truly that simple.

USING ALL THE STRATEGIES

You must utilize all available strategies for a very basic reason: if you rely upon one too much, your competition will quickly be able to see your next move. They will gain the upper hand, anticipating your actions and deftly avoiding your attacks.

The marketplace is ever-changing. Various strategies and methods of attack will fall in and out of favor depending on the environment you find yourself in. This harkens back to the idea of terrain. The pass at Thermopylae was an intense force multiplier for the Greeks; it would have been foolish for them to utilize a direct assault strategy with their limited numbers and superior positioning. Their surrounding environment and situation dictated their tactics.

You must always be aware of the operating environment of your business. For example, at the current moment, a major paradigm shift across all employment sectors is occurring. The 2008 crisis wiped out many jobs, but most of these positions have yet to come back—despite the US stock market rebounding to greater heights than ever before. The reason for this is quite simple: these jobs have been automated or were otherwise redundant. They are not coming back.

As an entrepreneur, this means that a wealth of reasonably priced labor is available without contract, on a freelance basis. Subscribing to the old paradigm—which means that you must have a central office, a dozen employees, and a cadre of other expensive accoutrements—would be disastrous. Your competitors are no doubt slashing costs, realizing that they can do business far quicker and cheaper when fewer people report to them.

Do not see things as you wish them to be. Unemployment is unfortunate, and many are struggling; nonetheless, you cannot wish for a return to the days of old, the golden ages of America's middle class. That was a different battlefield; the one where we find ourselves currently is craggy, shrouded in shade, with many places for clever, opportune individuals to lie in wait, earn victory through their nimbleness and bootstrapping capabilities.

The internet has opened up profound guerilla marketing and other advertising benefits—no longer must you spend thousands on ad spreads in a glossy magazine. You can start a business with zero upfront capital and be profitable within the week. While such a notion might seem fanciful—and yes, it is indeed a stretch—it is no longer an impossibility. Those lurking in the trees will find themselves looking down upon the proverbial Red Coats, the old guard proving to be easy pickings.

You can see this in numerous industries: the music, book and movie businesses being excellent examples. For years, these businesses exploited consumers with outrageous prices, bogus marketing tactics and other terrible methods of attack. When the indie revolution came—along with the rise of easy piracy—these entities tried to engage in a direct attack. They lined up their lawyers, refused to slash prices and continued their exploitation of customers.

They lost, and they will almost surely cease to exist within the next two decades—at least in their current form. They lost to people with far less resources, experience and other skills at their disposal. They lost because they refused to acknowledge their environment. They used old strategies, ones that made them billions in past years.

And they were all but buried in a manner of a few years.

If there's one universal truth of business and life, it is this: everything changes. As Sun Tzu wrote more than two millennia ago, "Do not be bound by convention, but give rewards as they are merited, and issue orders according to the situation."

You must always be adjusting. Most believe that the stone is more powerful than the rock; but, over time, water will wear away even the sturdiest granite, leaving behind nothing but a stream—placid, calm and entirely in control.

CHAPTER 6: Coaching and FURTHER READING

I offer assistance to entrepreneurs in the form of one on one coaching through my Entrepreneur Mentorship Program. So why do you need a coach? Well, even the great ones have had a coach to help them achieve the optimum level of success. NBA great Michael Jordan had Phil Jackson, baseball great Derek Jeter had Joe Torre, Olympic swimmer and multiple gold medalist Michael Phelps had Bob Bowman and Tiger Woods had Hank Haney.

None of the people mentioned here did it on their own. Sure they had the skills, drive, talent and put in the necessary hard work to achieve success, but they didn't do it on their own, they had a coach. If coaching helped them become great at what they do then it offers you those same benefits.

As your coach I will help you to:

- Clarify your vision
- Develop a Killer plan for your business
- Establish your goals
- Execute your strategies
- Make more money than you could ever dream of
- Show you how to crush the competition

For more information just visit

http://www.makeprofitseasy.com

Further Reading

There are many classic military texts; here are but a few that will help you on your journey. These are not based intensely on specific tactics; these books are more about the mindset of war and the warrior. In that way, they are applicable to all, even those who will never set foot on an actual battlefield. Let's first start off with my book which some are already calling a classic entitled The Killer Instinct: How To Master It and Achieve Anything You Want. The others are as follows:

The Art of War by Sun Tzu – a classic, and a must-read.

The Book of 5 Rings by Miyamoto Musashi – written by a samurai master, this is about how one cultivates discipline and the warrior's mindset.

The 33 Strategies of War by Robert Greene – a modern examination of military strategy, and how to use it in the modern world.

In addition to my book **The Killer Instinct: How To Master It and Achieve Anything You Want**, I have written other books that are available on Kindle, paperback and audio that you will find useful and helpful. **They are the following:**

How To Transform Yourself From Employee To Online Entrepreneur: Escaping The 9 To 5 Wage Slave Syndrome

Money Talks Bullshit Walks: The Entrepreneur's Guide to Productivity and Making More Money By Eliminating Distractions, Time Thieves and People Who Are Full of Shit

Winning Habits: Getting Rid of A Loser's Mentality

Conquering Your Fears

Passive Income: Stop Working Hard For Your Money And Let Your Money Work Hard For You

How To Create A Profitable Ezine From Scratch

The Secrets Of Making $10,000 on Ebay in 30 Days

The Complete Guide To Investing in Gold And Silver: Surviving The Great Economic Depression

How To Sell Any Product Online:"Secrets of The Killer Sales Letter"

Smart Money: How To Get Out Of The Consumer Trap And Invest Your Money Wisely

How To Make A Fortune Using The Public Domain

Search Engine Domination: The Ultimate Secrets To Increasing Your Website's Visibility And Making A Ton Of Cash

Creative Real Estate Investing Strategies And Tips

How to Make Money Online:"The Savvy Entrepreneur's Guide To Financial Freedom"

How to Overcome Your Self-Limiting Beliefs & Achieve Anything You Want

The Secrets of Finding The Perfect Ghostwriter For Your Book

The Creative Real Estate Marketing Equation: Motivated Sellers + Motivated Buyers = $

How To Start An Online Business With Less Than $200

How To Market Your Business Online and Offline

Money Blueprint: The Secrets To Creating Instant Wealth

Affiliate Cash: How To Make Money As An Affiliate Marketer

How To Promote Market And Sell Your Kindle Book

AudioBook Profits: How To Make Money by Turning Your Kindle, Paperback and Hardcover Book into Audio.

The Fine Art of Writing The Next Best Seller on Kindle

Fast Cash: 9 Amazing Ways To Make Money Without Having To Work At A Job

Money Magnet: How to use the Laws of the Universe to Attract Money into Your Life

Hypnotic Influence: How To Create A Cult Like Following For Anything That You Do

The Art of Manipulation: How to Get Anybody to Do What You Want

Jobless Cash: How to Make Money if You're Unemployed or Just Plain Tired of Working for Someone Else

What They Didn't Teach You In School About Money

Good luck and I wish you much success with your entrepreneurial endeavors and crushing the competition.

Sincerely,

Omar Johnson